The Aztec Empire

SUNITA APTE

Children's Press®
An Imprint of Scholastic Inc.
New York Toronto London Auckland Sydney
Mexico City New Delhi Hong Kong
Danbury, Connecticut

Content Consultant

Antonio Curet, Ph.D

Associate Curator, The Field Museum

Chicago, Illinois

Library of Congress Cataloging-in-Publication Data

Apte, Sunita.
  The Aztec Empire / by Sunita Apte.
        p. cm.—(A true book)
  Includes index.
    ISBN-13: 978-0-531-25227-7 (lib. bdg.)   978-0-531-24108-0 (pbk.)
    ISBN-10: 0-531-25227-2 (lib. bdg.)   0-531-24108-4 (pbk.)

  1. Aztecs—Juvenile literature. I. Title.

F1219.73.A68 2010
972'.018—dc22   2009000299

1 2 3 4 5 6 7 8 9 10 R 19 18 17 16 15 14 13 12 11 10   62

Find the Truth!

Everything you are about to read is true *except* for one of the sentences on this page.

Which one is **TRUE**?

T or F   In Aztec society, everyone wore gold jewelry.

T or F   The language of the Aztecs is still spoken today.

Find the answers in this book.

Sculpture of an Aztec warrior

Aztec calendar

Contents

THE BIG TRUTH!

Aztec mask

The Great Temple

Moctezuma II

There were 12 Aztec emperors between 1325 and 1521 C.E.

Sculpture of the Aztec god of music

The Aztec military kept the rulers powerful by conquering different areas, opening trade routes, and capturing enemies to offer them to the gods.

CHAPTER 1

Wandering People

Over 700 years ago, a wandering group of hunters and gatherers, called the Aztecs (AS-teks), settled in the Valley of Mexico, which is located in central Mexico today. They built a grand city and conquered the other groups of people living around them. Eventually the Aztecs created a great **empire** and accomplished many amazing things.

 Aztec warriors used animals such as an eagle and a jaguar to represent themselves.

Settling for Greatness

According to Aztec legend, the Aztec people **originated** in the northern part of Mexico. Around 1100 C.E., they left their homeland and wandered for several centuries, looking for a place to settle. Wars with other groups of people may have forced the Aztecs to keep moving. Around 1250 C.E., the Aztecs finally settled in the Valley of Mexico and began building their empire.

Although the Aztec Empire existed hundreds of years ago, its people were able to establish an impressive capital city, build a strong army, develop a written language, and create art and poetry. Experts have learned much about the Aztecs' accomplishments by studying their documents and ruins.

The Aztecs used a 365-day calendar, just like we do today.

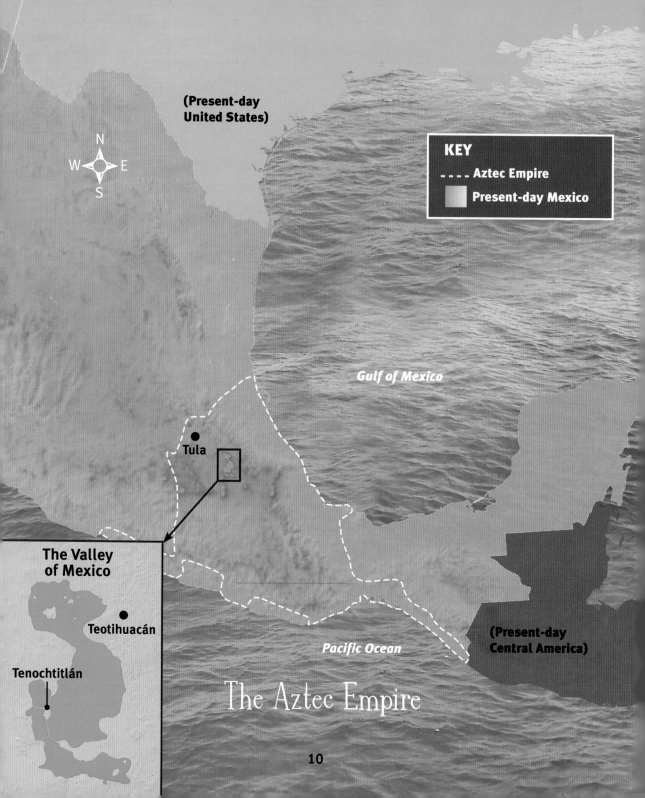

(Present-day
United States)

N
W · E
S

KEY
- - - - Aztec Empire
⬛ Present-day Mexico

Gulf of Mexico

● Tula

**The Valley
of Mexico**

● Teotihuacán

Tenochtitlán

Pacific Ocean

(Present-day
Central America)

The Aztec Empire

CHAPTER 2

The Valley of Mexico

The Valley of Mexico is a **fertile** region that once included five lakes. The Aztecs settled there around 1250 C.E. In and around the lakes, the Aztecs could hunt and fish. Over time, they learned how to work the valley's land and became skilled farmers. In addition to the Aztecs several different ancient peoples lived throughout the region in **city-states**.

← The Aztec people were originally known as the Mexica (meh-SHEE-kah).

Before the Aztecs

About 2,000 years ago, the Valley of Mexico was the site of a great ancient city known as Teotihuacán (tay-oh-tee-wah-KAHN). This city was powerful for almost a thousand years, but not much is known about the people who built it and lived there. Eventually, Teotihuacán declined and a group of people called the Toltecs (TOLL-teks) took over. They were great warriors, artists, and thinkers. The Toltecs ruled over the Valley of Mexico for more than 200 years.

Giant Toltec figure

Tenochtitlán

Island City

When the Aztecs arrived in

Today, Lake Texcoco is mostly dried up.

the Valley of Mexico, more powerful groups of people were already living there. Because of this, the Aztecs were forced to build their city on an island in the middle of swampy Lake Texcoco (TEKS-koh-koh). Since their city was surrounded by water, it should have been easy for other groups to attack. Instead, the Aztecs were actually protected by the water around them. Soon their city, Tenochtitlán (teh-nock-teet-LAHN), was the most powerful in the Valley of Mexico.

CHAPTER 3

The Center of an Empire

The city of Tenochtitlán was the capital of the Aztec Empire. More than 200,000 people lived there. To make Tenochtitlán so great, the Aztecs used what they learned from the other groups of people that had lived in the Valley of Mexico.

There were many temples and palaces in the center of Tenochtitlán.

The Aztecs traveled by boat to sell fruit and animals.

Roads, Canals, and Markets

Along with its stone palaces and temples, Tenochtitlán had large roads built over water, called causeways. These causeways connected the city to Lake Texcoco's shore. The city also had many canals. Boats brought people and goods from the shore to Tenochtitlán, or from one part of the city to another. Tenochtitlán also had a very large market stocked with food and crafts.

Aztec Foods

The ancient Aztec diet included corn tortillas,
tomatoes, chili peppers, beans, squash, avocados,
and turkey. The cacao (kuh-KAY-oh) seed, from
which chocolate is made, was very important to
the Aztecs. The seeds were combined with spices
and peppers to make a drink like hot chocolate.
Only wealthy Aztecs were allowed to drink it.
Since cacao trees didn't grow well in the Valley of
Mexico, the seeds
were brought in
from far away.
The seeds were
so valuable that
they were often
used as money.

**The seeds used by the
Aztecs are found inside of
a cacao bean like this one.**

Aztec Gods

Religion was very important to the Aztecs and they worshipped many gods. The main Aztec god was Huitzilopochtli (wee-tsee-loh-POHCH-tlee), the god of war. Other gods included Tlaloc (tlah-LOHK), the god of rain and water, Chicomecoatl (chee-koh-meh-KOH-tull), the goddess of corn, and Quetzalcoatl (ket-sahl-koh-AHT-l), the god of life and nature. Throughout the empire, there were temples dedicated to each god.

Quetzalcoatl

Quetzalcoatl means "feathered serpent".

Tlaloc, the god of rain and water, could bring life-giving rain but also deadly lightning and floods.

At the temples, priests led the Aztecs in worship of the gods by saying prayers, playing music, and giving gifts called offerings. In their homes, people worshipped the gods at small **altars** containing wooden statues. The Aztecs believed that the gods held power over every part of their lives. They prayed to win battles, to catch lots of fish, and to harvest large crops of corn.

Aztec rulers wore headdresses made from the feathers of the quetzal (KET-zal) bird.

A Supreme Ruler

The Aztecs were led by a ruler called a *tlatoani* (tla-toe-AHN-ee). A *tlatoani* had complete and unlimited power over the government and army and ruled for life. When he died, one of his relatives was chosen to be the new *tlatoani*. Acamapichtli (ah-kah-mah-PITCH-tlee) became the first *tlatoani* in 1375 C.E. Under its first six rulers, the Aztec Empire grew and became very powerful. By the time the ninth *tlatoani*, Moctezuma (mawk-te-SOO-mah) II, came to power, the Aztec Empire covered more than 80,000 square miles (207,200 square kilometers).

Different groups
of Aztec society

Citizens of the Empire

There were three main groups of people in Aztec society. The *macehualtin* (mah-say-WALL-teen) were the common working people. They included farmers and craftsmen. The *pochteca* (poch-TA-ca) were traders and the *pipiltin* (pee-PEEL-teen) were Aztec nobles and lords. The *pipiltin* had special rights that weren't granted to the *macehualtin*. Only the *pipiltin* could wear clothes made out of cotton and jewelry made out of gold.

The Great Temple at Tenochtitlán

The Great Temple was in the center of Tenochtitlán. It was also the religious center of the Aztec world. The temple was dedicated to Huitzilopochtli, the god of war and the sun, and to Tlaloc, the god of water and rain. At the Great Temple, Aztec priests performed ceremonies and made offerings to honor the gods.

Hidden for Centuries

While digging in a Mexico City street in 1978, workers found a huge carved stone that was an artifact from the Aztec Empire. They had actually discovered the site of the Great Temple of Tenochtitlán.

Sacred Site

The Great Temple was the tallest building in Tenochtitlán. From the top, an Aztec ruler could see for miles. The Aztecs believed that the temple's height made it closer to the gods.

This is what a marketplace may have looked like in Tenochtitlán.

Life in Tenochtitlán

By studying ruins and writings, experts have learned a lot about the daily lives of the Aztecs. The emperor or *tlatoni* and nobles lived very differently from most people. The emperor lived in an elegant palace and had fine clothes. Common people were forced to give him food and goods as a kind of tax. It was believed that these donations were a way to honor the emperor. For most Aztec people, days were filled with hard work.

 More than 50,000 people visited the markets in Tenochtitlan every day.

Farming

Aztec farmers worked hard to grow crops for Tenochtitlán. Many of them took care of sections of land called *chinampas* (chee-NAM-pahs). *Chinampas* were very fertile islands of farmland that were built in Lake Texcoco around Tenochtitlán. The Aztecs created these islands by piling layers of plants and mud on the lake's bottom. Building these *chinampas* and growing food on them was very hard work.

Aztecs building a *chinampa*

26

Home Life

Aztec women looked after their homes and prepared food. An Aztec woman might have spent much of her day weaving or grinding corn to make tortillas. Most Aztec women learned how to weave at a young age so they could make clothes for their families. Aztec women might have also woven

In some parts of Mexico today, women grind corn just as Aztec women did hundreds of years ago.

capes that were sold at Tenochtitlán's large and busy market.

A Writing System

The Aztecs spoke Nahuatl (nah-WAH-duhl), a language that is still used in some parts of Mexico today. They also had a writing system made up of symbols known as **glyphs** (GLIFFS). Each glyph could represent part of a word, a person, place, object, or idea. The Aztecs wrote on long sheets made of cloth, tree bark, or animal skins. These sheets were used to make a kind of book called a **codex** (KOH-deks). By studying many Aztec books, or codices (KOH-dih-sees), experts have learned much about Aztec life.

One of the most famous Aztec codices is known as the Codex Mendoza.

Aztec Games

The Aztecs liked to play games. *Patolli* (pah-TOLL-ee) was a popular board game. Players threw dice made from dried beans and moved game pieces on an X-shaped board. For a game called *Ullamalitzli* (ooh-lah-mah-LEETS-lee) players used their elbows, knees, hips, heads, and shoulders to pass a rubber ball around a special court. Experts believe that Aztec warriors may have played this game to prepare for war. It's also thought that this game was played to act out the battle between the forces of life and death or light and darkness.

Patolli board game

This painting shows the first meeting between the Spanish leader, Hernán Cortés, and the Aztec ruler, Moctezuma II.

CHAPTER 5

The End of an Empire

After 200 years in power, the Aztec Empire came to a sudden end. In 1519 C.E., the Spanish explorer and conqueror Hernán (er-NAHN) Cortés (kawr-TEZ) arrived in Mexico. Cortés was searching for new lands that Spain could conquer. He brought 500 Spanish soldiers in three ships to help him accomplish his mission.

The Aztecs may have at first believed that Cortés was the god Quetzalcoatl.

Preparing to Invade

By 1519 C.E., Moctezuma II had ruled the Aztecs for 17 years. However, nothing had prepared him for the strange visitors who arrived from Spain. Moctezuma II sent **ambassadors** (am-BASS-uh-durs), or representatives with gifts, to meet them. Cortés forced the ambassadors to watch as a cannon was fired. The Aztecs were afraid of this giant weapon. Cortés knew that the ambassadors would go back to Moctezuma II and describe what they had seen. He wanted Moctezuma II to fear him.

Cortés began to march his army toward Tenochtitlán to conquer the Aztecs and take over the Valley of Mexico for Spain. When he stopped in towns along the way, Cortés learned that some people were unhappy with Moctezuma II.

The Aztec people hated paying taxes to the empire. So Cortés invited them to join him and his soldiers. He knew he would need more fighters if he wanted to overthrow Moctezuma II and take control of the empire.

Moctezuma II

Friends and Enemies

Moctezuma II did nothing to stop Cortés and his army. Instead, he treated the Spanish like royal guests when they arrived in Tenochtitlán. Moctezuma II showed Cortés all of Tenochtitlán and even gave him a tour of the Great Temple. But Cortés hadn't changed his mind about conquering the Aztecs.

Cortés accepts gifts sent by Moctezuma II.

34

There were many battles between the Spanish and the Aztecs.

He made Moctezuma II a prisoner and took charge of Tenochtitlán. Cortés and his soldiers looted the city, stealing gold and other treasures.

Soon afterward, Cortés had to return to the Gulf of Mexico coast. He left some soldiers behind to watch over the city. These soldiers treated the Aztecs very badly, and fighting broke out between them. It only got worse when Cortés returned to Tenochtitlán. The battles grew more brutal and deadly. In one of them, Moctezuma II was killed.

After the attack on Tenochtitlán, Cortés took Cuauhtémoc prisoner to find out where his gold was.

36

After Moctezuma II's death, Cortés and his soldiers left the city. Aztec warriors chased them and many soldiers died. Over the next year, Cortés built up his army so he could begin conquering the Aztec Empire again.

In May of 1521 C.E. , Cortés and his army returned to Tenochtitlán. They found the city to be a very different place. Smallpox, a disease brought by the Spanish, had spread through the city. Tens of thousands of Aztecs had died from the disease. Even though Tenochtitlán was already very weak, it took Cortés months to conquer the city. Finally, on August 13, 1521 C.E., the Spanish captured the Aztec's new ruler, Cuauhtémoc (kwoh-TEH-mock). The great Aztec Empire had come to an end.

Today, Mexico City is one
of the largest cities in the world.

CHAPTER 6

The Spanish Take Control

Once Cortés took control of Tenochtitlán, the whole Aztec Empire became a Spanish **colony**. As a colony, the Aztecs were ruled by the government of Spain. The Spanish controlled the Valley of Mexico for 300 years. During that time, the lives and traditions of the Aztecs would be changed forever.

Mexico's capital, Mexico City, is built on top of Tenochtitlán.

Spanish Rule

Government officials and other people sailed over from Spain to settle the new colony. Many of these people came looking for gold that would make them rich. Others came to teach the Aztecs about religion. The Spanish built a new city on top of Tenochtitlán. They constructed churches over the Aztec temples and destroyed many Aztec codices. Treasured gold objects were sent back to Spain where they were melted down. Some Aztec gold was even used to decorate Spanish churches.

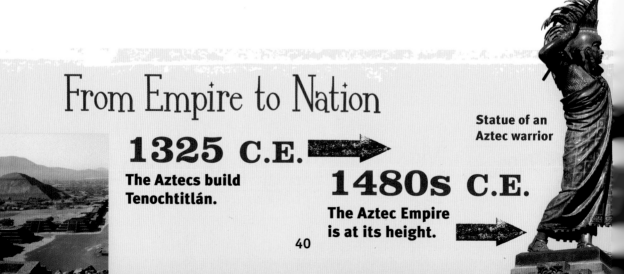

From Empire to Nation

1325 C.E. ➡
The Aztecs build
Tenochtitlán.

1480s C.E.
The Aztec Empire
is at its height. ➡

Statue of an
Aztec warrior

The eagle and serpent on the Mexican flag represent the country's Aztec roots.

The new Europeans who moved to the Valley of Mexico brought more diseases with them. They forced the Aztecs to work difficult and dangerous jobs. All of this proved deadly for many Aztecs. When Cortés had first arrived in the Valley of Mexico, over a million people were living there. Sixty years later, only about 200,000 Aztecs were left.

1521 C.E.

Cortés conquers Tenochtitlán. 41

1821

Mexico gains its independence from Spain.

The Aztec Past

After a long struggle, Mexico finally won its independence from Spain in 1821. By then, much of the Aztec **culture** had vanished. But reminders of Mexico's Aztec past still survive today. About a million people still speak Nahuatl, the Aztec language. And many important ancient Aztec sites and ruins can be found throughout Mexico. Today, experts continue to study and learn more about the great Aztec Empire. ★

The Aztecs built this circular temple in what is now Toluca, Mexico, to honor the wind god.

True Statistics

Number of people in the Aztec Empire:
About 10 million

Number of Aztec calendars: 2

Aztec symbols on the Mexican flag: An eagle and a serpent fighting on a cactus

Date Tenochtitlán was founded: 1325 C.E.

Size of Tenochtitlán: 5 square mi. (13 square km)

Number of Aztec rulers: 11

Important Aztec rulers: Acamapichtli: 1375–1395; Itzcoatl: 1427–1440; Moctezuma I: 1440–1469; Ahuitzotl: 1486–1502; Moctezuma II: 1502–1520

Part of an Aztec calendar

Did you find the truth?

F In Aztec society, everyone wore gold jewelry.

T The language of the Aztecs is still spoken today.

Resources

Books

Baquedano, Elizabeth. *Aztec, Inca & Maya.* New York: DK Publishing, 2005.

Conklin, Wendy. *Mayas, Aztecs, Incas.* New York: Scholastic Teaching Resources, 2006.

Jolley, Dan. *The Smoking Mountain: The Story of Popocatépetl and Iztaccíhuatl: An Aztec Legend.* Minneapolis, MN: Graphic Universe, 2008.

Lourie, Peter. *Hidden World of the Aztec.* Honesdale, PA: Boyds Mills Press, 2006.

Macdonald, Fiona. *You Wouldn't Want to Be an Aztec Sacrifice!* New York: Franklin Watts, 2001.

Sonneborn, Liz. *The Ancient Aztecs.* New York: Franklin Watts, 2005.

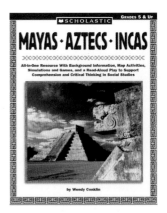

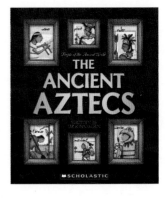

Organizations and Web Sites

PBS: Conquistadors
www.pbs.org/conquistadors
Learn more about Hernán Cortés, the man who conquered the Aztec Empire.

Kidspast.com
www.kidspast.com/world-history/0281-aztecs.php
Read all about the Aztec Empire.

Aztec History
www.aztec-history.com/index.html
Discover facts about Aztec weapons, war, jewelry, and much more at this site.

Places to Visit

American Museum of Natural History
Central Park West and 79th Street
New York, NY 10024-5192
(212) 769 5100
www.amnh.org
Explore the architecture and art of the Aztecs in the Hall of Mexico and Central America.

The Field Museum
1400 South Lake Shore Drive
Chicago, IL 60605-2496
(312) 922 9410
www.fieldmuseum.org
See a full-sized replica of the Sun Stone in the Ancient Americas exhibit.

Important Words

altars – places, usually tables, where religious objects are kept

ambassadors (am-BASS-uh-durs) – people who represent the government to foreigners

artifact – an object that was made by people, such as a tool or weapon

city-states – cities and the villages around them that had their own independent government

codex (KOH-deks) – a book made from writing on a sheet of cloth, animal skin, or tree bark

colony – a region ruled by a government that is far away

culture – the language, ideas, and art of a particular group of people

empire – many different people, groups, or countries under the control of one ruler or government

fertile – able to produce crops

glyphs (GLIFFS) – picture symbols used in writing

originated – started or came into being

Index

Page numbers in **bold** indicate illustrations.

About the Author

Sunita Apte has written over 40 fiction and nonfiction books for kids. When she is not writing books at home in Brooklyn, New York, Sunita loves to travel the world with her family. Mexico is one of her favorite places to visit. The ancient sites there never cease to amaze her.